# THE SECRET TO GETTING WHAT YOU WANT:

## *10 Steps to Teen Success*

by Lee Stein

the paradoxical press

Published by The Paradoxical Press, Teaneck, NJ

Please visit The Paradoxical Press at www.theparadoxicalpress.com

Library of Congress Cataloging-in-Publication Data

Stein, Lee, 1970-
  The secret to getting what you want : 10 steps to teen success / by Lee Stein.
      p. cm.
  ISBN 978-0-9786663-1-6
  1.  Success in adolescence. 2.  Interpersonal communication in adolescence.
  3.  Interpersonal relations in adolescence. 4.  Conduct of life.  I. Title.
  BF724.3.S9S74 2011
  155.5--dc22
2011003145

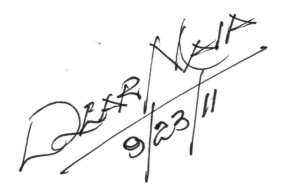

*To my boys,*
*who always keep me laughing*

# Contents

# Introduction

*You're a teenager – you're busy – you've got places to go and people to see and homework to finish and games to play and friends to call and parents to drive crazy. Like I said … busy! That's why this book is short and sweet and to the point.*

*But don't let the modest page count fool you. Inside this 100-page book are the key principles to getting what you want. Once you learn them you will understand why those who use them succeed, and those who don't often fail.*

*This book is not about reinventing the wheel. The principles outlined here may seem obvious to you; you may have heard them before … from your parents or even your kindergarten teacher. But somewhere along the way life got complicated, our priorities shifted, and many of these fundamental principles got lost in the shuffle.*

**The Secret to Getting What You Want** *is about going back to the basics in order to build for yourself the best possible future. As a teenager, you now have the wisdom, maturity, and presence of mind that you did not possess as a child, and with these you can begin to refine your character and decide what kind of an impact you want to have on the world around you.*

---

I've learned from experience that the greater part of our happiness or misery depends on our dispositions and not on our circumstances.
**Martha Washington, First Lady, United States of America, 1731 – 1802**

Our attitude toward life determines life's attitude toward us.
**Earl Nightingale, Motivational Speaker and Author, 1921 – 1989**

# The Golden Rule

You may have heard of the Golden Rule ... in a sermon, in a book, or in a conversation. It's a principle or philosophy held by a wide variety of cultures and religions, dating all the way back to Hammurabi, the sixth king of Ancient Babylonia, circa 1700 bce. It has been taught in different languages, using different words and different metaphors, but the principle remains the same: **treat others as you wish to be treated**.

The principles of communication found in this book are a reflection, or incorporation, of the Golden Rule. If you think about it, our lives – our *functionality* – all boil down to communication. We are communicating every second of the day: with our faces, with our bodies, with our words, and with our actions. When we give charity, we're communicating to the recipient that we care about his well-being. When we talk on the phone or text with a friend, we're communicating our interest in that person's life. When we sit in a classroom, our behavior communicates how interested or uninterested we are in the subject matter. All too often, though, we communicate before we think. We make a gesture or we blurt something out before we consider how it will affect the other person.

As you read through the principles in this book, I recommend first thinking about how you would feel if those around you adopted these values and used them in their daily interaction with you. If you think your relationships and your communication with these people would improve tremendously, then I hope you will understand the benefit of adopting these principles yourself.

What better way to lead by example than to exemplify the most positive traits a human being can have? What better way to create positive energy than to eliminate the negative habits you have developed over time? What better way to make yourself memorable and carve out a successful future for yourself than to emulate the practices of some of the most admired and respected figures in the world?

You will notice that the principles in this book are also actions. To become the person you want to be, it's not enough to believe you can be a better person. The choices you make and the actions you take are what will define you and your character. Read this book and learn from it, but more importantly, let it motivate you to take the steps you need to create a better life for yourself and for those around you.

Before you read any further, I'd like you to decide what kind of a person you want to be. Then take out a piece of paper and write a list of words that you would like others to use when describing you (e.g., kind, friendly, sincere, helpful, etc). Leave a line or two between each word and, as you read the chapters in this book and learn how to create effective communication and relationships with those around you, refer back to that list and write a sentence or two about how you plan on becoming this person. Are you going to help out around the house? Encourage others when they've lost hope? Consider someone else's opinion as seriously as your own? Only you can fill in those lines for yourself because ultimately you are the decision-maker when it comes to your character.

CHAPTER 1

# IF YOU WANT TO LIVE LONGER

Let us make one point, that we meet each other with a smile, when it is difficult to smile.

**Mother Teresa, Worldwide Humanitarian and Nobel Peace Prize Winner, 1910 – 1997**

Wear a smile and have friends; wear a scowl and have wrinkles. What do we live for if not to make the world less difficult for each other?

**George Eliot, Prolific Author, 1819 – 1880**

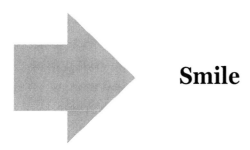

# Smile

Take a moment and try this little experiment. Put a big smile on your face and say the following: "Sometimes life really gets me down. I don't know who my real friends are and sometimes I feel lonely." Felt awkward didn't it? That's because it's hard to feel down when you have a big smile plastered on your face.

A smile is a very powerful thing. It changes your body language, tells people you're happy, and can even make them wonder what they can do to be as happy as you. People who smile are thought to be better communicators, better managers, and even better parents. In fact, many psychologists believe that if you smile first, positive feelings will follow. That's right … your physical state of being affects your emotional state of mind – not the other way around. You can't laugh without a smile, and you know what they say … laughter is the best medicine.

You would never think of frowning at the person who is meeting you for an interview, so why frown at your friends and family, the people you really care about? Why be known as a grouch when you can develop the reputation of a friendly, approachable person with a great attitude? And how about going one better and making someone else smile? If you can turn a person's frown into a smile, you could make a friend for life.

---

## Top 7 Reasons to Smile
## adapted from Mark Stibich, Ph.D.

Smiling is a great way to make yourself stand out while helping your body to function better. Smile to improve your health, your stress level, and your attractiveness. Smiling is free and it's a fun way to live longer!

**Someone who smiles lightens up the room**

 ### *Smiling Makes Us Attractive*

We are drawn to people who smile. There is an attraction factor. We want to know a smiling person and figure out what is so good. Frowns, scowls and grimaces all push people away, but a smile draws them in.

**2** ### Smiling Changes Our Mood

Next time you're feeling down, try putting on a smile. There's a good chance your mood will change for the better. Smiling can trick the body into helping you change your mood.

**3** ### Smiling Is Contagious

Someone who smiles lightens up the room and can even change the moods of others. Smiling people bring happiness with them. Smile often and you will draw people to you.

**4** ### Smiling Relieves Stress

Stress can really show up in our faces. Smiling helps to prevent us from looking tired, worn down, and overwhelmed. When you are stressed, take time to put on a smile. You'll reduce your stress and feel better able to take action.

**5** ### Smiling Boosts Your Immune System

Smiling helps the immune system to work better. When you smile, immune function improves, possibly because you're more relaxed. Prevent the flu and colds by smiling.

**6** *Smiling Releases Endorphins, Natural Pain Killers, and Serotonin*

Studies have shown that smiling releases endorphins, natural pain killers, and serotonin. Together these three make us feel good. Smiling is a natural drug.

**7** *Smiling Makes You Seem Successful*

Smiling people appear more confident, more approachable, and achieve their goals faster than others.  Put on a smile at school, on interviews, and at work and people will react to you differently.

CHAPTER 2

# BUT ENOUGH ABOUT YOU

You can make more friends in two months by
becoming interested in other people
than you can in two years by trying to get
other people interested in you.
**Dale Carnegie, Pioneer of Self
Improvement and Best Selling Author,
1888 – 1955**

The meeting of two personalities is like the
contact of two chemical substances:
if there is any reaction, both are transformed.
**Carl Jung, Psychoanalyst, 1875 – 1961**

# Express Interest In Other People

D o you know who you spend most of your time thinking about? If you guessed "ME" you're correct! Most people are interested in themselves above anyone else. But do you know who is *most liked* by everyone? Those who express a greater interest in others, above themselves. It is truly a special person who can put aside his or her own thoughts and feelings for a time and make an effort to really get to know someone else. Not only is it a great way to learn new things, but it's a sure way to make new friends.

Can you think of a time when you felt important because someone asked you a question you knew the answer to, or someone came to you for advice? It probably made you feel good to help that person and to know they trusted you. To feel important is one of our strongest desires. When we express interest in other people we help satisfy that need and, in turn, we experience the satisfaction of giving unselfishly.

Would you like to see people take an interest in the things you say and do? Then take the first step and ask them about themselves! Be sincere, be enthusiastic, and be attentive. Remember, you've had your whole life to get to know yourself. Take some time to learn something new from somebody new ... express an interest in other people.

## 10 Simple Ways to Show Your Sincere Interest in Others,
### by Todd Smith, Entrepreneur, Author, and Founder of Little Things Matter

1. *Make your greeting stand out* – Whether you meet people for the first time or greet them for the tenth time, you have an opportunity to make a positive impression. The key here is to take ten seconds and make them feel like the most important people on this earth. Look them in the eyes with warmth and authenticity and offer them a friendly greeting. If appropriate, give them a firm handshake or hug.

2. *Use names* – In all of your communication, written or verbal, first time or repeated, make it a point to use a person's name. In Dale Carnegie's timeless book *How to Win Friends and Influence People* he wrote, "If you want to win friends, make it a point to remember them. If you remember my name, you pay me a subtle compliment; you indicate that I have made an impression on you. Remember my name and you add to my feeling of importance."

**③ _Listen with interest_** – There is a difference between simply listening to people and listening with deep interest. Listening with interest signifies that you really care about what they are saying in contrast to simply listening because it's the polite thing to do. If you question whether people can tell the difference, DON'T. They can and they will readily make judgments about you if they sense you are pretending to listen.

**④ _Ask questions_** – A great way to demonstrate interest is to ask questions. It could be as simple as striking up a conversation with a co-worker about what they did over the weekend, or perhaps asking something about her family. Asking questions generally stimulates a person to talk about her interests and herself.

**⑤ _Acknowledge people_** – When you acknowledge people, you recognize their value and importance. How about hugging your children before they go off to school? Or saying "good morning" to your co-workers as you walk through the office? Or saying "hi" to an acquaintance you see dining at another table in a restaurant? When you go out of your way to acknowledge people you will make a positive impression on them.

**⑥ _Show respect_** – When you show people respect, your actions express your interest in them. Think about it.

When people show you respect, how does it make you feel about them (and about yourself)? On the other hand when people DON'T show you respect, how do you feel about them?

**7** ***The old fashioned way*** – One of the best ways to demonstrate the importance of a relationship is to call someone just to see how he's doing. I receive very few calls from people who don't have a self-serving agenda. Those who call because they genuinely care about me stand out in my mind. How frequently do people call you just to say "hi" or find out what's going on in your life? How does that make you feel?

**8** ***Offer genuine compliments*** – When people take the time to offer you a sincere compliment, how does that make you feel about them? Are you naturally drawn to people who speak positively of you? When you take an extra ten seconds to offer people a genuine compliment, your interest in them can have a far greater impact than you realize.

**9** ***Encourage people*** – When you encourage others, you lift their spirits, enhance their self-confidence, and add fuel to their motivational fire. Perhaps more than anything you give them hope and inspiration. Wow! If simple words of encouragement can do so much to enhance someone's life, why don't we all do more of it? How long could it take? Ten seconds?

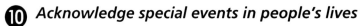**Acknowledge special events in people's lives**
– When you make the effort to remember important
dates in people's lives, be it birthdays, anniversaries,
religious holidays, or even the anniversary of a loved
one's death, your efforts make a personal and long-
lasting impression.

CHAPTER 3

# WHAT DID YOU SAY?

It is the province of knowledge to speak. And it is the privilege of wisdom to listen.

**Oliver Wendell Holmes, American physician, poet, and humorist, 1809 – 1894**

Listening, not imitation, may be the sincerest form of flattery.

**Dr. Joyce Brothers, noted psychologist, columnist, author, and radio personality, 1928 – present**

# Be A Good Listener

When you listen to what people say you are doing much more than just listening. You are showing them you care about what they have to say (whether you agree or not), showing them respect, being a person they can talk to, and letting them express themselves.

The most successful businesspeople in the world will tell you that listening is the key to achievement. If we don't listen to others, we can't learn about their needs. And if we can't learn about their needs, how will we ever satisfy them?

Have you ever wondered why telemarketers are so unpopular? You might think it's because they call at dinnertime. But if I called you at dinnertime to tell you about the new car I've decided to give you, I don't think you'd be in such a rush to hang up the phone, would you? The real problem with telemarketers is that they don't take the time to learn whether we have a need for their company's product *before* trying to sell it to us. And when you think about it, it's awfully presumptuous to try to sell something to people before you've determined whether they even have a need for it.

17

Similarly, it's much easier to give personal advice to friends once you know what their problems are. And the only way – *the one and only way* – to learn what the problem is, is to listen. By looking at them directly when they speak to you (and not glancing off in every direction), by responding appropriately (instead of "mmhm" and "yeah"), and by expressing a genuine interest in what they have to say, you are validating their thoughts and feelings. Think about the person you always go to when you need to talk. Take

> **The most successful business people in the world will tell you that listening is the key to achievement.**

a little time to figure out what makes him a good listener, and think about how important you feel when he listens to you. If you can keep that feeling in mind when someone is talking to you, you are on your way to becoming a good listener.

---

## Adapted from
### *Are You a Good Listener?*
**by John Milton Fogg, Author of *The Greatest Networker in the World***

Research shows that just about 85 percent of all we know we learned by listening. Yet the same studies tell us that we are "distracted, preoccupied or forgetful" more than 75 percent of the time, and at best we remember only 20 percent of what we actually hear!

Furthermore, the average person listens at a rate of between 150 and 250 words per minute, but thinks at a rate of 1000, 2000, 3000 words and more! Simple physics tells us that no two things can take up the same space at the same time and because "thoughts are things," it's just not possible to be thinking away at a couple of thousand words a minute and still hear what another person is saying.

The following quiz itemizes 11 ways in which we may not be paying as close attention as we could be when someone is addressing us. If you can identify what you are doing instead of really listening to the other person, you can change the outcome of any communication for the better, and perhaps, once you make a habit of *really listening,* you can change your life and the lives of many others for the better.

---

## The Listening Quiz

Here are 11 ways you may not hear what other people are saying. Rate yourself from one of the following five choices and learn what kind of a listener you've been up until today.

〇Never  〇Occasionally  〇Sometimes  〇Frequently  〇Always

**1** *Comparing* – Comparison is competition, and you never want to compete with your friends, customers, spouse, children or anyone else. Who's right and who's wrong? Who cares? It's a conversation! Just listen. And of course, stay away from any assessment about the messenger and focus simply and completely on hearing the message.

**When I listen to other people I am *comparing* ...**

⃝ Never  ⃝ Occasionally  ⃝ Sometimes  ⃝ Frequently  ⃝ Always

**2** *Derailing* – The easiest way to deliver a clear "I don't care about what you're saying" (and, therefore, you!) communication is to change the subject, knocking the other person off-track before she's finished. If you're not sure if the other person is finished speaking, wait a few seconds and watch her face to see if more is forthcoming. Look her in the eye and say, "Is it OK if I say something?" or "I'm a little uncomfortable with the subject matter. Is it OK if we speak about something else?"

**When I listen to other people I *derail*...**

⃝ Never  ⃝ Occasionally  ⃝ Sometimes  ⃝ Frequently  ⃝ Always

**3** **Dreaming**

"Excuse me, what did you say?"

"Would you repeat that?"

"What? Sorry, I wasn't listening."

These are all perfect ways to make the speaker feel unimportant and insignificant. Sometimes you'll want to think about something someone has just said. If this is the case, just stop the conversation right there and say, "Wait a minute, Mary, I want to think about what you just said." Saying that is a great acknowledgment. The other person will both respect you and love you for it!

**When I listen to other people I am *dreaming*...**

O Never   O Occasionally   O Sometimes   O Frequently   O Always

**4** *Fighting* – What could be more disturbing and off-putting than to hear your conversation partner say, "My dog's better than your dog" or any variation of that playground theme? If you want to make a sure and fast enemy, disagree, disapprove, challenge, belittle, begrudge, put down, or power over the person who's talking. But if you want to dialog in a mature manner, respectfully tell this person that you heard what he has to say and you have a different view on the matter. Disagreeing is a part of communication, but listening shows your partner that, above all, you respect his right to have an opinion.

When I listen to other people I am *fighting*...

O Never   O Occasionally   O Sometimes   O Frequently   O Always

**5** *Filtering* – We are all a product of our own unique education and, as such, we will always see and hear the world through our own individualized lens. It's difficult to listen to what others say without filtering their words through our personal experiences, attitudes, positions, points of view, and opinions. But when we do that, are we truly hearing them? Or are we really just holding up their words to our own one-of-a-kind judgment and evaluation? The next time you listen, try setting aside your own internal commentary. If you don't, all you'll ever hear is yourself.

When I listen to other people I am *filtering*...

O Never    O Occasionally    O Sometimes    O Frequently    O Always

**6** *Identifying* – You've heard the term "Great minds think alike," but in actual fact great minds disagree more often than not. That's how great minds grow great: they explore different ideas, challenge their own perceptions, and entertain new directions. It's fun to discover a like-minded or similar-feeling friend, but rushing to agree with him could mean you're not really listening. Rather, you could be selectively hearing what you identify with and filtering out the rest. Be aware of how you listen and be sure to stay true to what you believe.

When I listen to other people I am *identifying* ...

O Never    O Occasionally    O Sometimes    O Frequently    O Always

**7** *Interpreting* – Here's a profound yet perplexing truth: we make it all up. When someone says "blue" what color comes to your mind? Dark blue, light blue, navy blue, royal blue? Everything is an interpretation. Even two scientists observing the same precise experiment can reach different conclusions. Here's a classic example of interpreting:

Person A: "Does the blue in this shirt remind you of the sky?"

Person B: "Not at all!" (assuming that Person A does not want a sky-blue colored shirt)

Person A: "Oh, that's too bad. I love sky blue shirts."

The 11th Commandment: Thou shalt not interpret. Instead, just listen and find out what the speaker really means.

When I listen to other people I am ***interpreting*** …

O Never  O Occasionally  O Sometimes  O Frequently  O Always

**8** ***Mind Reading*** – Oscar-winning director and playwright Mike Nichols said, "You'll never really know what I mean and I'll never know exactly what you mean." We can't read each other's minds just as we can't know each other's thoughts and feelings. If we did, communication would become obsolete. It's OK to be empathetic, and you can still be on each other's wave length; but it's always better to listen to what the other person has to say than to assume you already know.

When I listen to other people I am ***mind reading*** …

O Never  O Occasionally  O Sometimes  O Frequently  O Always

**9** ***Placating*** – When someone continuously nods her head, agreeing with everything you say, how does that make you feel? Are you secure and at ease, or do you think "I wish she would stop yessing me all the time and get her own opinion!"? Avoiding disagreement or conflict by putting on a people-pleasing-personality tends to send others in just the opposite direction. They lose their respect and their trust in you because they feel you're being insincere. If you don't know what to say, just listen.

When I listen to other people I am ***placating*** …

O Never  O Occasionally  O Sometimes  O Frequently  O Always

**10** ***Plotting*** – If you already have a plot in mind for the conversation you're having– like the structure of a novel or a drama – you're not listening. You're too involved in directing the conversation to fit with your plot to hear what the other person is really saying. Plotting can also indicate an ulterior motive, a hidden agenda in which you want to control the outcome of the conversation. Either way, it's impossible for the other person to be genuinely heard. Practice listening without an agenda. Instead of trying to manipulate the other person to see it your way, simply listen for a good "fit." A good fit means you're not trying to fit a square peg (his opinion) into a round hole (your opinion).

When I listen to other people I am ***plotting*** …

O Never  O Occasionally  O Sometimes  O Frequently  O Always

**⑪** *Rehearsing* – You cannot hear someone, even just a little bit, when you're thinking about what you're going to say next. A listener who's more interested in herself and what she has to say can barely wait for the other person's last word to be uttered before jumping in to respond. This kind of behavior can make others feel small and insignificant. The next time someone is speaking to you, listen and validate (what she has said). Do not listen and violate (her desire to be heard).

When I listen to other people I am ***rehearsing*** ...

◯Never  ◯Occasionally  ◯Sometimes  ◯Frequently  ◯Always

There is no official score chart here. Rather, take note of your answers and continually strive to tune in to, or focus on, those who are speaking to you.

# CHAPTER 4

**JUST**
~~DO IT~~
**DON'T**
**DO IT**

I have yet to find the man, however exalted his station, who did not do better work and put forth greater effort under a spirit of approval than under a spirit of criticism.

**Charles Schwab, Brokerage Industry Pioneer, founder of Charles Schwab & Co., 1937 – present**

Don't find fault, find a remedy.

**Henry Ford, founder of the Ford Motor Company, 1863 – 1947**

"Being kind is more important than being right."

**H. Jackson Brown Jr., Author of the best selling "Life's Little Instruction Book," 1940 – present**

# Do Not Criticize

The bite, the sting, the pain of being criticized. We have all felt it and we know all too well that it rarely corrects the problem. Why, then, do we so readily partake in it ourselves? The answer is less complicated than you might think. It's the solution, however, that proves challenging.

We criticize people for all sorts of reasons: because they did it incorrectly, because they didn't do it the way we would have done it, because we think we know better, because we think we know best. We criticize because, unfortunately, it's easier to focus on what's wrong rather than what's right; because it is easier to react without thinking, rather than thinking about how to react. How often does the victim of a critical remark chuckle and respond with, "You're right, I completely messed up"? More likely, as humans are prone to do, that person becomes defensive, tries to justify his actions, and bears ill will toward the one who has made him feel small and inept. In the end, criticism rarely solves the problem – but it can create many more.

The next time you feel like jumping down someone's throat, take a moment to ask yourself: What is the reason this mistake occurred? How would I have reacted in this situation? What will I succeed in doing by criticizing this person? Is it really my place to judge?

No one is perfect, least of all ourselves. Try to remember that before dealing the next blow to someone's ego. Chances are she has already berated herself for making a mistake and criticizing her is more likely to turn her embarrassment into anger.

## HOW TO OFFER CONSTRUCTIVE CRITICISM

➤ ***Instead of criticizing, try suggesting.*** A suggestion can be seen as constructive and unpresumptuous … more useful than criticism.

➤ ***Be positive.*** Instead of using negative terms such as "don't" and "can't," try using positive terms such as "can" and "will" and "I feel good about…"

➤ ***Be specific.*** The more specific you are, the more confident the other person will feel about meeting your expectations. Try emphasizing what you specifically like (versus don't like) about the work that's been completed so far.

➤ ***Show compassion.*** Put yourself in the other person's shoes for a moment and try to figure out how you would want to be approached in the same situation. What would you want to hear? What method of communication would help you respond in the most positive way? Try beginning with a compliment and ending with a compliment to keep the conversation even keeled.

➤ ***Don't criticize the person.*** Criticize the action or behavior you want to correct. Instead of saying "You didn't use a nice color" try "I'd love to see this in a different color."

## HOW TO ACCEPT CRITICISM GRACEFULLY

▶ ***Respond ... don't react.*** It's perfectly natural to feel defensive when someone has criticized you or your work, but lashing out will only make things worse. Take some time to let your emotional reaction wash over you and allow reason to settle in its place. A cool and calm response will win you more respect than an angry and passionate one.

▶ ***Don't take it personally.*** You drew a red circle. Your boss wants it in blue. No one is right or wrong here, you simply have different tastes. When you own the company you'll get to choose the color! In the meantime, recognize that his taste isn't better, it's just not the same as yours.

▶ ***Pluck the positive from the negative.*** Forget for a moment who is criticizing you and why. Be brutally honest and ask yourself what part of that feedback you can really learn from. What part of that criticism resonates with you so that you are forced to look at it from all angles and admit to yourself that there's something you can be doing better?

▶ ***Say thank you.*** Just because Mr. Bitter Bones doesn't know how to communicate effectively with others doesn't mean you should forget your manners. In fact, remaining humble in the face of adversity often softens our critics and reminds them that there's a better way to communicate their opinion.

▶ ***Rise above.*** There will always be snarky critics who feel better by making you feel worse. When this happens just remind yourself how thankful you are that that's not you. Every day you can choose to be nice to people or mean to people. Be proud of the fact that you choose to be positive!

CHAPTER 5

# HOW MANY TIMES A DAY DO *YOU* DO IT?

Never tell evil of a man if you do not know it for certainty, and if you know it for a certainty, then ask yourself, "Why should I tell it?"
**Johann K. Lavater, German poet and physiognomist, 1741 – 1801**

Fire and swords are slow engines of destruction, compared to the tongue of a Gossip.
**Richard Steele, 18th century Irish writer and politician, 1672 – 1729**

I think the hardest part about being a teenager is dealing with other teenagers – the criticism and the ridicule, the gossip and rumors.
**Beverley Mitchell, American actress and country singer, 1981 – present**

Whoever gossips to you will gossip about you.
**Spanish Proverb**

# Do Not Gossip

Reputations – even lives – have been destroyed by gossip. Our words have the power to heal but also to wound. Gossip has become such standard conversation that most of us don't even realize we're doing it. When we look in the mirror and say things like, "I'm fat" or "I'm ugly," we are gossiping even about ourselves! For this reason, among many others, "do not gossip" is one of the toughest principles of all to follow.

Imagine a world where we are all satisfied with who we are and what we have. This world would be virtually unrecognizable to us because we live in an age where consumers collectively spend billions of dollars each year on plastic surgery to change their physical appearance and even more billions of dollars visiting psychologists and psychotherapists trying to find happiness.

It's no wonder we're so drawn to gossiping about others. This nasty habit not only shifts our focus away from what we personally do not have, but it also ensures that we are not alone in our misery by dragging others down with us. If I can make somebody cry or feel small, I can feel superior or in better control of my life.

The problem with gossip is that it may offer some temporary relief and distraction from our lives (and the more we do it the more often we feel this relief, thus its addictive nature), but it doesn't address the heart of the problem – the reason we gossip in the first place.

We live in a world where perfection is defined by the glamorous images we see on TV. We know these images have been manipulated ... by plastic surgery, by Photoshop, by makeup, and more. We know these images are not real, yet we continue using them to set the bar in our own lives. This irony makes self-acceptance virtually impossible. If the perfection we seek to obtain is based on a lie, it can never truly be achieved.

In order to eradicate the need and the desire to gossip, *which is a symptom of the lack of this false "perfection" in our lives,* we need to break the spell we are under by rejecting the image of perfection the media have created for us and realizing that the key to happiness and satisfaction is accepting ourselves as we are.

Remember that elusive world where we are all satisfied with who we are and what we have? That world will exist when we recognize that there is no authority on what's beautiful and what's ugly because everything simply "is what it is." When we begin accepting ourselves and others for who they are, negative words and gestures will disappear.

## The Way It Is:

Lisa used to date Brian. They broke up a month ago but she still has feelings for him. Brian has started dating the new girl, Sabrina, and Lisa can't help but feel jealousy and animosity toward Sabrina. Lisa begins spreading rumors about Sabrina, claiming she stole Brian away from her and that she sleeps around. Suddenly, people Sabrina doesn't even know start giving her dirty looks, calling her names, and making her feel miserable. Brian still likes her but his friends are pressuring him to break up with her because she has a bad reputation. Sabrina can't walk the school halls anymore without people trying to shame her ... she no longer wants to get up in the morning.

## The Way It Should Be:

Lisa is sad that Brian broke up with her, but she knows what a great person she is and, besides, she doesn't want to be with someone who doesn't want to be with her! When Lisa sees that the girl Brian wants to date is Sabrina, she realizes that Brian wasn't looking for someone better, just different. Sabrina seems like a nice girl, but they have very different looks and personalities. Lisa notes that she misses having a boyfriend but it's time to move on and find someone she is more compatible with.

# CHAPTER 6

# TO EACH HIS OWN... AGENDA

If I have ever made any valuable discoveries, it has been owing more to patient attention than to any other talent.

**Sir Isaac Newton, renowned scientist and mathematician, 1642 – 1727**

The two most powerful warriors are patience and time.

**Leo Tolstoy, Russian novelist, War and Peace, Anna Karenina, 1828 – 1910**

# Exercise Patience

**B**eing patient can be a challenge! Sometimes when we want something, we want it immediately and it's hard to wait. We often overlook the fact that what's important to us is not as important to others.

Do you remember how it felt the last time you asked for something, or just wanted someone's attention, and you were told you would have to wait? Perhaps you started to whine or cry or tap your feet to let the other person know you were waiting impatiently.

People who lack patience often let their temper get the best of them and often cause others to lose their temper. If you can picture everyone getting worked up and upset and nobody at all getting what they want, you might be able to appreciate the value of being a patient person.

The next time you want something and your mom or dad or friend is too busy to give it to you, remember that by giving them the time they need to finish what they're doing, you're showing them the patience and appreciation you are sure to get in return when they're ready to address you.

The next time someone needs *your* attention and you're tempted to put him on hold, think about the power you have to make that person feel important just by exercising a little patience. Put your needs aside for one moment, smile, and look him in the eye. Show someone you care about his needs as much as you care about your own.

**We often overlook the fact that what's important to us is not as important to others.**

Force someone to give you what you want and she will do so reluctantly. Allow someone the time to attend to your needs, and she will do so graciously and with a smile. This is what is meant by "good things come to those who wait."

---

In Buddhism, patience is the sixth of the ten perfections (the virtues one has to perfect in order to fully awaken, live an unobstructed life, and reach the goal of enlightenment).

Buddhists believe that patience is motivated by our desire for inward and outward peace and by faith in our ability to accept things as they are. In Buddhism patience has three essential aspects: gentle forbearance, calm endurance of hardship, and acceptance of the truth.

## The first aspect of patience is **gentle forbearance.**

- Forbearance means refraining from something or exercising self-control.
- If you feel yourself growing impatient (e.g., with a friend's non-stop chatter or a frustrating work assignment) take a few deep breaths instead of yelling in frustration.
- Gentle forbearance helps us restrain ourselves long enough to determine the most skillful action for the moment.
- Gentle forbearance includes the spirit of forgiveness. When we feel conflict with others, understanding their suffering is the first step in being able to communicate, forgive, and begin again.
- The practice of forgiveness happens when we are able to realize the underlying cause of our anger and impatience. This allows us to distinguish between someone's unskillful behavior and essential goodness.

## The second aspect of patience is the **calm endurance of hardship**.

- We develop patience by learning to accept and have compassion for suffering rather than trying to eradicate it.

43

- When we feel impatient with our relationships, our work, or our spiritual practice, we need to realize that we are resisting how things are.
- A sense of humor and curiosity about our lives can also help us confront impatience.
- In a frustrating situation, it helps to ask ourselves the question, "How would I benefit from being patient right now?" The answer may be that in taking a deep breath and slowing yourself down, you will notice things you would have missed by rushing around.
- Remember to practice relaxing in your life, in all its joys and sorrows, and to relinquish the need to know what's going to happen next.

The third aspect of patience is
**acceptance of the truth**.

- This means that we accept our experience as it is – with all its suffering – rather than how we want it to be. As we come to this understanding, we gain the strength to be present for the long haul, and we are less likely to get caught in being overly insistent, frustrated, and demanding.
- There is great power in patience because it cuts through arrogance and ingratitude. Holding on to our judgments about others and ourselves is a major cause of impatience.

- Repeating softly to ourselves, "May I be happy just as I am" and "May I be peaceful with whatever is happening" helps us accept our vulnerabilities, imperfections, and losses.

- By accepting the agreeable and disagreeable aspects of life, we are no longer limited by our longing for life to be different than it is. We have all the time in the world, in the spaciousness of every moment.

CHAPTER 7

# A BASIC HUMAN NEED

Giving people self-confidence is by far the most important thing that I can do.  Because then they will act.

**Jack Welch, CEO General Electric,**

**1935 – present**


The way to develop the best that is in a man is by appreciation and encouragement.

**Charles Schwab, Brokerage Industry**

**Pioneer, founder of Charles Schwab & Co.,**

**1937 – present**

# Give Encouragement

If you always had the choice to make someone feel good or feel bad, which would you choose? People look for encouragement every day. In fact, one of our most basic human needs is to believe that the things we do are important and have meaning. It's a unique trait that distinguishes humans from animals (that, and opposable thumbs!).

It feels good when someone tells you what a great job you've done, doesn't it? How often do you take the time to give someone else that same kind of encouragement? We all know people who find it easier to see the bad things in life rather than the good things, who find it easier to put people down rather than pay them a compliment, who prefer to say, "That's easy, I could do that!" rather than "Wow – you're very talented." It's possible that these people were not given a lot of encouragement growing up, and as a result they do not believe in themselves. These people need an extra dose of encouragement to feel special – so why don't you try giving it to them? In fact, I'd like to *encourage* you to try to convince all the people you know that they're special! Tell them what good friends they are to you; tell them the project they're working on looks great; tell them what you think they're really good at and how you wish you could do it as well as they can.

Not only will people think you're special for saying such positive things, but there's a good chance that they too will learn how to become positive people who can provide you with encouragement whenever and wherever you need it.

---

## Adapted from:
## How to Encourage the SMART way, by Daphne Lim at www.joyfuldays.com

While trying to figure out how to give meaningful encouragement, I realized that the acronym "SMART" used for goal-setting, was quite useful. Here's how to apply the SMART approach to encourage others.

 ## Specific

While any praise feels good, there is greater impact when the person knows exactly what he did well. Consider the difference between being vague and being specific in the following examples:

*Vague: "You did well on that project."*

**Specific: "You chose a really catchy name for that project. I can't get it out of my mind."**

*Vague: "Your teacher says you're a good student."*

*Specific: "Your teacher says she's very happy that you always hand in your work on time."*

 ## Measurable

Even if the person knows exactly what he did well, he may not realize why it's so important to you. Giving him feedback *in measurable terms* will make your praise more meaningful.

*"You chose a really catchy name for that project. I can't get it out of my mind. **I'll be sure to remember it the next time I need inspiration for my own projects.**"*

*"Your teacher says she's very happy that you always hand in your work on time. **It saves her the trouble of having to remind you and gives her ample time to go through your assignments in detail.**"*

 ## Action

When you praise a person's character, he may get a warm fuzzy feeling but there's not much he can do after that. When you praise an action instead, you encourage him to repeat that same positive behavior.

*Character: "You are a valuable employee."*
*Action: "You chose a catchy name for that project."*

*Character: "You are such a good student."*
*Action: "You hand in your work on time."*

## Relevant

We sometimes give encouragement that is neither here nor there. "You look nice today" isn't as effective as encouragement that is specific to your friend's goals. Relevant encouragement is more helpful to that person by nudging her in the direction she wants to go rather than distracting her from it.

GOAL: GET A PROMOTION AT WORK.
*Irrelevant: "You chose a really catchy name for that project. You should consider a career in advertising."*

**Relevant: "You chose a really catchy name for that project. I bet the bosses will pay attention when you present it at next week's meeting."**

GOAL: IMPROVE GRADES IN SCHOOL.
*Irrelevant: "It's great that you hand in your work on time because it gives you more time to play once the work is done."*

*Relevant: "It's great that you hand in your work on time because planning ahead allows you time to plan and produce quality work which can get better results."*

## Timely

Books on dog training say that the best time to give your dog a treat is immediately after she has completed the task you have asked of her. If you offer the treat later she won't connect the reward to the action and you won't be reinforcing that specific behavior..

Human nature does not differ too much in this regard. Studies show that the best time to give encouragement for an action is when the person is still experiencing an emotional connection to that action. Children seem to know this – they ask for their promised reward as soon as they've performed the deed. Your timely encouragement can enhance that emotion and stimulate the formation of synapses in the mind, reinforcing the person's memory of, and motivation to, repeat the action. Be sure to offer encouragement as immediately as you can in order to have the greatest impact.

CHAPTER 8

# THE
# HALL
# OF
# SHAME

A person who publicly shames his neighbor is
like someone who has shed blood ...
Indeed, I have seen that when someone is
shamed, the color leaves his face and he
becomes pale.
**Talmud**

Isn't it kind of silly to think that tearing
someone else down builds you up?
**Sean Covey, Author of *The 7 Habits of***
***Highly Effective Teens***

# Do Not
# Embarrass Others

**M**ost people I know do not embarrass others intentionally. They do it with a wisecrack to make others laugh, or they blurt something out impulsively, not thinking about how or whom it may offend. There are also those whose popularity is measured by how many people they can embarrass. As the number of people they belittle increases, so does the crowd of people who surround them to share in the laughter. But do you think it's really a popularity contest this person has won? Do you think the crowd that surrounds him and snickers along is thinking, "Wow, what a great friend?" Of course not! They simply crowd around this person who sits on his high horse in an effort to avoid embarrassment themselves.

What a shame it is that in order for some people to feel good they must make others feel bad, that for a good laugh they will completely disregard another's feelings and sensitivities. The fear of embarrassment lives within us all – some of us will even lie or blame others in order to avoid it! And yet, when it comes to embarrassing others,

> **What a shame it is that in order for some people to feel good they must make others feel bad.**

how often do we really take the time to consider the blow we will be delivering to someone's confidence by calling attention to his faults?

The next time you think you have something witty to say about another person, ask yourself first if that comment is going to make that person feel good or bad, make her seem smart or silly, or make you feel better or worse for saying it. Ask yourself how you would feel if someone were to say the same thing about you. If you do not like the answer, you can learn to refrain from embarrassing others.

---

## Excerpt from Dick Gregory's
### *Nigger: An Autobiography*

I never learned hate at home, or shame. I had to go to school for that. I was about seven years old when I got my first big lesson. I was in love with a little girl named Helene Tucker, a light-complexioned little girl with pigtails and nice manners. She was always clean and she was smart in school. I think I went to school then mostly to look at her. I brushed my hair and even got me a little old handkerchief. It was a lady's handkerchief, but I didn't want Helene to see me wipe my nose on my hand...

Everybody's got a Helene Tucker, a symbol of everything you want. I loved her for her goodness, her cleanness, her popularity. She'd walk down my street and my brothers and sisters would yell, "Here comes Helene," and I'd rub my tennis sneakers on the back of my pants and wish my hair wasn't so nappy and the white folks' shirt fit me better. I'd run out on the street. If I knew my place and didn't come too close, she'd wink at me and say hello. That was a good feeling. Sometimes I'd follow her all the way home, and shovel the snow off her walk and try to make friends with her momma and her aunts. I'd drop money on her stoop late at night on my way back from shining shoes in the taverns. And she had a daddy, and he had a good job. He was a paperhanger.

I guess I would have gotten over Helene by summertime, but something happened in that classroom that made her face hang in front of me for the next twenty-two years. When I played the drums in high school, it was for Helene, and when I broke track records in college, it was for Helene, and when I started standing behind microphones

> **I never learned hate at home, or shame. I had to go to school for that.**

and heard applause, I wished Helene could hear it too. It wasn't until I was twenty-nine years old and married and making money that I finally got her out of my system. Helene was sitting in that classroom when I learned to be ashamed of myself.

It was on a Thursday. I was sitting in the back of the room, in a seat with a chalk circle drawn around it. The idiot's seat, the troublemaker's seat.

The teacher thought I was stupid. Couldn't spell, couldn't read, couldn't do arithmetic. Just stupid. Teachers were never interested in finding out that you couldn't concentrate because you were so hungry, because you hadn't had any breakfast. All you could think about was noontime; would it ever come? Maybe you could sneak into the cloakroom and steal a bite of some kid's lunch out of a coat pocket. A bite of something. Paste. You can't really make a meal of paste, or put it on bread for a sandwich, but sometimes I'd scoop a few spoonfuls out of the big paste jar in the back of the room. Pregnant people get strange tastes. I was pregnant with poverty. Pregnant with dirt and pregnant with smells that made people turn

**The teacher thought I was stupid. Couldn't spell, couldn't read, couldn't do arithmatic. Just stupid.**

away. Pregnant with cold and pregnant with shoes that were never bought for me. Pregnant with five other people in my bed and no daddy in the next room, and pregnant with hunger. Paste doesn't taste too bad when you're hungry.

The teacher thought I was a troublemaker. All she saw from the front of the room was a little black boy who squirmed in his idiot's seat and made noises and poked the kids around him. I guess she couldn't see a kid who made noises because he wanted someone to know he was there.

It was on a Thursday, the day before the Negro payday. The eagle always flew on Friday. The teacher was asking each student how much his father would give to the Community Chest. On Friday night, each kid would get the money from his father, and on Monday he would bring it to the school. I decided I was going to buy a daddy right then. I had money in my pocket from shining shoes and selling papers, and whatever Helene Tucker pledged for her daddy I was going to top it. And I'd hand the money right in. I wasn't going to wait until Monday to buy me a daddy.

I was shaking, scared to death. The teacher opened her book and started calling out names alphabetically: "Helene Tucker?" "My Daddy said he'd give two dollars and fifty cents." "That's very nice, Helene. Very, very nice indeed."

That made me feel pretty good. It wouldn't take too much to top that. I had almost three dollars in dimes and quarters in my pocket. I stuck my hand in my pocket and held on to the money, waiting for her to call my name. But the teacher closed her book after she called everybody else in the class.

I stood up and raised my hand.

"What is it now?"

"You forgot me?"

She turned toward the blackboard. "I don't have time to be playing with you, Richard."

"My daddy said he'd..."

"Sit down, Richard, you're disturbing the class."

"My daddy said he'd give...fifteen dollars."

She turned around and looked mad. "We are collecting this money for you and your kind, Richard Gregory. If your daddy can give fifteen dollars you have no business being on relief."

> All she saw from the front of the room was a little black boy who squirmed in his idiot's seat and made noises and poked the kids around him.

"I got it right now, I got it right now, my Daddy gave it to me to turn in today, my daddy said..."

"And furthermore," she said, looking right at me, her nostrils getting big and her lips getting thin and her eyes opening wide, "We know you don't have a daddy."

Helene Tucker turned around, her eyes full of tears.

She felt sorry for me. Then I couldn't see her too well because I was crying, too.

"Sit down, Richard."

And I always thought the teacher kind of liked me. She always picked me to wash the blackboard on Friday, after school. That was a big thrill; it made me feel important. If I didn't wash it, come Monday the school might not function right.

"Where are you going, Richard!"

I walked out of school that day, and for a long time I didn't go back very often.

CHAPTER 9

# LOSE THE BATTLE, WIN THE WAR

Behind every argument is someone's ignorance.

**Louis D. Brandeis, Supreme Court Judge, 1856 - 1941**

I can win an argument on any topic, against any opponent. People know this, and steer clear of me at parties. Often, as a sign of their great respect, they don't even invite me.

**Dave Barry, Humor Columnist and Best Selling Author, 1947-present**

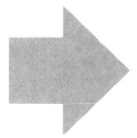

# Avoid Arguments

Can you remember the last time you argued with someone, raised your voice, or told her she was wrong? What do you remember from that argument? Was it the thrill of winning? Proving your point? Making a new friend? Most likely it was none of those things. In fact, if you are like most people, that argument probably resulted in little more than hard feelings. Great friendships have been lost because of a single argument, the subject of which has been long forgotten by both injured parties.

Arguments are usually about egos, about making the other person feel small so that you can feel tall. Take a minute to think about the last argument you engaged in and ask yourself the following questions:

- Did anything good come of it?
- Did I earn this person's respect or resentment?
- Would the result have been different if we had respectfully agreed to disagree instead of forcing our opinions on one another?

Consider the following two people:

**Great friendships have been lost because of a single argument**

**Person A** feels very strongly about his opinion. He raises his voice, stamps his feet, and says things like, "Don't be ridiculous!" and "How can you possibly think that way?" He wants to argue until the other person is forced to agree with him. He feels triumphant when he is the winner.

**Person B** also feels strongly about his opinion but he knows that others might disagree. He smiles and says things like, "I hear what you're saying. I have a different understanding of this subject and I'd like to know what you think." He states his opinion and then welcomes the other person's feedback. If he and the other person cannot reach an agreement he graciously says, "It sounds like we have different opinions on this matter but I've learned a lot from you on this subject."

Which person would you prefer to disagree with? Which person would you like to be? If you answered Person B then consider the following: Instead of rushing to discredit the next person who disagrees with you, and instead of punching holes in this person's opinion (and ego), first ask yourself:

Is arguing with this person really necessary? If I listen to her and express appreciation for her opinion, isn't it more likely that I can expect the same in return? Can I find something in her opinion to agree with in order to engage her from a positive approach? Am I willing to admit when I'm wrong and not stubbornly cling to my ideas? Do I want people to perceive me as an argumentative person who cannot reason, or a person who is interested in what others have to say and respects their right to say it without interruption or reproach?

If you can remember that your friends don't have to be wrong for you to be right, and that someone does not have to lose in order for you to win, then you can do what millions of other people cannot ... avoid arguments.

---

## How to Keep a Disagreement from Becoming an Argument

**excerpted from** *How to Win Friends and Influence People*, **by Dale Carnegie, quoting from** *Bits and Pieces*, **published by The Economic Press**

**Welcome the disagreement.** When two partners always agree, one of them is not necessary. Perhaps this disagreement is your opportunity to be corrected before you make a serious mistake.

**Distrust your first instinctive impressions.** Our first natural reaction in a disagreeable situation is to be defensive.  Be careful.  Keep calm and watch out for your first reaction.  It may be you at your worst, not your best.

**Control your temper.** You can measure the size of a person by what makes him or her angry.

**Listen first.** Give your opponents a chance to talk. Let them finish.  Do not resist, defend or debate.  This only raises barriers.  Try to build bridges of understanding. Don't build higher barriers of misunderstanding.

**Look for areas of agreement.** When you have heard your opponents out, dwell first on the areas in which you agree.

**Be honest.** Look for areas where you can admit error and say so.  Apologize for your mistakes.  It will help disarm your opponents and reduce defensiveness.

**Promise to think over your opponents' ideas and study them carefully.** Your opponents may be right.  It's a lot easier at this stage to agree to think about their points than to move rapidly ahead and find yourself in a position where your opponents can say "We tried to tell you, but you wouldn't listen."

**Thank your opponents sincerely for their interest.** Anyone who takes the time to disagree with you is interested in the same things you are.  Think of them as people who really want to help you, and you may turn your opponents into friends.

**Postpone action to give both sides time to think through the problem.** Suggest that a new meeting be held later that day or the next day, when all the facts may be brought to bear. In preparation for this meeting, ask yourself some hard questions:

Could my opponents be right? Partly right?

Is there truth or merit in their position or argument?

Is my reaction one that will relieve the problem, or will it just relieve any frustration?

Will my reaction drive my opponents further away or draw them closer to me?

Will my reaction elevate the estimation good people have of me?

Will I win or lose?

What price will I have to pay if I win?

If I am quiet about it, will the disagreement blow over?

Is this difficult situation an opportunity for me?

CHAPTER 10

# SAY IT LOUD, SAY IT CLEAR

There's a song that goes '"Sorry seems to be the hardest word."'. But it's not the words that are difficult. It's meaning them. And not stopping until the injured party believes you do.

**Mitch Albom, best-selling author, newspaper columnist and radio host, 1958-present**

When armies are mobilized and issues are joined, the man who is sorry over the fact will win.

**Lao-Tzu, Chinese Taoist Philosopher, (604 BC - 531 BC)**

# Learn To Say "I'm Sorry"

I'm sorry. Two magical words, yet two of the hardest words for people to say. Why? Simply because "I'm sorry" is an admission of guilt. Whether you accidentally bumped into someone, intentionally insulted her, or unintentionally offended her – there she stands in front of you, hurt – and there you stand feeling mighty small for making her feel bad. "Sure I'm sorry," you're thinking. "I feel terrible. Isn't it obvious? And now I have to say I'm sorry? I just want to pretend like it never happened!"

I, I, I … me, me, me … when you're feeling small it's hard to think about anyone but yourself and your bruised ego. But let me tell you a little secret – a magical two-word secret. "I'm sorry" makes the pain go away. "I'm sorry" allows a person to forgive *and* move on. "I'm sorry" makes you feel tall, not small, stronger, not weaker. "I'm sorry" means you can make mistakes because you're only human, and be honest enough to admit when you're wrong.

When you say "I'm sorry," there's a good chance you will be forgiven. When you say "I'm sorry" quickly

> **"I'm sorry" means you can make mistakes because you're only human, and be honest enough to admit when you're wrong.**

and genuinely you can regain someone's trust in an instant. Ask yourself who is a stronger person: one who clings stubbornly to his pride and never backs down, or one who has the confidence to admit to himself – and to others – when he has done something wrong?

Next time you make the mistake of hurting someone, physically or emotionally, see how quickly you are able to defuse the situation with an effective and emphatic "I'm sorry!"

These two little words can change your life.

---

## 10 Ways To Say I'm Sorry

**1** Leave a note or a card for him inside his locker, car, gym bag … somewhere he's sure to see it.

**2** Treat her to dinner and dessert. Better yet, *cook* dinner and dessert for her!

**3** By him a CD of music he likes.

**4** Buy her flowers ... even just one flower can be effective.

**5** Bake him a cookie or cake and spell out "I'm Sorry" with chocolate chips.

**6** Make her a mixed CD with a lot of "I'm Sorry" and "I Love You" songs. There are plenty to choose from.

**7** Write him a poem about how you feel.

**8** Offer a hug

**9** (Fill this one in yourself)

**10** (Fill this one in yourself)

# Bonus Chapters

Although the following two bonus chapters do not speak directly to "communication" I feel very strongly that they affect our communication on a weekly, daily, even hourly basis. Communication is a two-way street. If we just wanted to hear the sound of our own voices, we could talk to a wall or some other inanimate object that can neither teach us nor learn from us. And what's the point of communicating if we're not teaching or learning something?

The *way* we communicate is just as, if not more, important than the information we're communicating. If you tried reading a bedtime story to a toddler by yelling and screaming each word while stomping your feet, do you think you will have achieved the true purpose of reading a bedtime story (to calm, comfort, and lull her to sleep)? Your attitude, or your state of mind, directly affects your ability to teach and to learn.

# Bonus Chapter 1:

Have you ever observed someone's poor behavior and thought, "I'm glad I'm not her"? Or maybe you watched a reality TV show and were inspired when ordinary people fought extraordinary odds and won. *Every day you learn how to behave and how not to behave, and this affects your attitude toward communicating with others.*

# Bonus Chapter 2:

Are you a "glass half empty" or a "glass half full" person? Study after study has shown that successful people are natural optimists. Where others dwell on limitations, they see opportunity. Who would you rather be when you go on that job interview, Mr. Limitations or Mr. Opportunity? *Your ability to maintain a positive outlook impacts the nature of your communication with others.*

# LEARN SOMETHING FROM EVERYONE

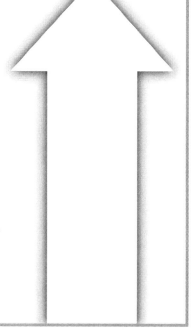

I have never met a man so ignorant that I couldn't learn something from him.
**Galileo Galilei, famous astronomer and physicist, 1564 – 1642**

I have learnt silence from the talkative, toleration from the intolerant, and kindness from the unkind.
**Kahlil Gibran, poet, philosopher, artist, 1883 – 1931**

If I am walking with two other men, each of them will serve as my teacher. I will pick out the good points of the one and imitate them, and the bad points of the other and correct them in myself.
**Confucius, famous Chinese philosopher, circa 551 – 479 B.C.**

# Learn Something from Everyone

We have been learning something from everyone since the day we were born: how to walk, how to talk, how to interact – in short, how to live. Along the way people started learning from us too – perhaps our younger siblings or our peers. But in the process of developing our intellect and learning how to form our own opinions, we began to take our mentors and instructors in life for granted. It's ironic – because our interaction with others is what teaches us about our likes and dislikes, what motivates us, what turns us off, what we are good at, and what we still have to learn.

If we were all the same – had the same thoughts and feelings and opinions – life would get pretty boring. Over the course of your life you are likely to meet hundreds of interesting and different people. Funny or serious, happy or sad, friendly or distant, one thing is for sure: the more people you meet, the more you will learn about life and about yourself. So instead of tolerating differences, let's learn to welcome and appreciate them.

If you have a tendency to discount people you don't

> **The more people you meet, the more you will learn about life and about yourself.**

like or with whom you have nothing in common, I would encourage you to take a closer look. Every person you meet has information and knowledge that you don't have, that you can use, now or in the future. Find out what it is and file it away. You never know when it will come in handy.

Don't take anyone in your life for granted! Take a moment to think and write down what you have learned from the following people (good or bad):

Mother: _____

_____

Father: _____

_____

Sister: _____

_____

Brother: _____

_____

Favorite teacher: _____

_____

Least favorite teacher: _____

_____

Salesperson in your favorite clothing store: _____

_____

Favorite TV character: _____

_____

Favorite actor/actress: _____

_____

Favorite author: _____

_____

Clergy (pastor, rabbi, imam): _____

_____

Boyfriend/Girlfriend:_____

_____

Mail carrier: _____

_____

Bus driver: _____

_____

Camp counselor: _____

_____

BONUS CHAPTER 2

# FIND THE GOOD ... IN EVERYTHING

We could never learn to be brave and patient
if there were only joy in the world.
**Helen Keller, world renowned ambassador
for the deaf and blind, 1880 – 1968**

You cannot tailor-make the situations in life
but you can tailor-make the attitudes to fit
those situations.
**Zig Ziglar, popular motivational speaker
and author, 1926 – present**

# Find the Good...
# in Everything

L ife has its share of ups and downs, but did you know that your *outlook* on life can easily affect its *outcome*?

Are you a positive or a negative person? Do you say things like, "You will!" "You can!" "You are!" or do you find yourself saying, "That's going to be tough." "This is impossible." "I'm just not good enough."? The problem with negative thoughts and energy is that they only lead to more negative thoughts and energy. Did you ever notice that when something bad happens your mind tends to wander to all the other bad things that have ever happened to you? It's a vicious cycle that can take you and your attitude to a very low place.

On the other hand, when you're feeling great and things seem to be going your way, you're not really bothered by small annoyances. You're experiencing all these great feelings and you have energy to pass along to your friends. How do you hold on to this feeling?

Like most other things, learning to think positively is something you can acquire through practice and commitment. Thinking positively doesn't mean you won't experience sadness or pain or loss, but it will affect your approach to these experiences. One very important principle to remember is that people and experiences will only affect you the way you allow them to affect you. This is because *you* have control over your emotions. It may not seem that way all the time, but remember: your best friend could never cheer you up if you really didn't want to feel better. In the end, it is *you* who choose to be happy again.

The next time something negative happens, remind yourself that you *can* choose to respond positively.

---

## Here are a number of tips to help you find the positive in everything.

### REPLACE NEGATIVE THOUGHTS WITH POSITIVE THOUGHTS

If you're watching a scary show on TV, don't turn the TV off and let that fear linger! Change the channel and quickly readjust your frame of mind. When you find yourself fixated on a negative image or incident, try to find one time in your life that you can always come back to, that you can rely upon, to bring a smile to your face.

### EVALUATE IT, LEARN FROM IT

Did someone hurt your feelings or take you for

granted? Perhaps someone close to you passed away or you've been feeling neglected. You've experienced the pain; now it's time to figure out what you can learn from it. Remember that at the very least, bad experiences can help you appreciate the good ones even more.

## SAY "THIS TOO IS FOR THE BEST" EVERY DAY

When you stub your toe, when you fail a test, when you get in trouble: figure out how this too is a positive thing. No matter how ridiculous, no matter how contrived, and no matter how impossible it may seem, search your mind for something – anything – that can turn this incident from a negative into a positive. If you force yourself to do this every day for a week, you will start doing it without even realizing it and you will have developed an invaluable habit.

## SAY "IT COULD BE WORSE"

Did you fail a test? Could be worse … at least you didn't flunk out of school. Did you sprain your ankle? Could be worse … at least you didn't break your leg. It might seem like a cliché, but challenge yourself to put things into perspective instead of blowing them out of proportion. Yes, life gets tough. But the choice is always yours: let your circumstances get the best of you, or rise above them.

**WATCH YOUR THOUGHTS,
FOR THEY BECOME WORDS.**

**WATCH YOUR WORDS,
FOR THEY BECOME ACTIONS.**

**WATCH YOUR ACTIONS,
FOR THEY BECOME HABITS.**

**WATCH YOUR HABITS,
FOR THEY BECOME
CHARACTER.**

**WATCH YOUR CHARACTER,
FOR IT BECOMES
YOUR DESTINY.**

# Positive Attitude Building Exercises

▶ At the end of each day, review the activities of that day and ask yourself if there was anything you could have done better or differently.

▶ Commit to paying a compliment to at least one person each day.

▶ Commit to paying yourself a compliment each day.

▶ Identify specific positive traits in others that you are drawn to and mirror them until they become your own.

▶ Make sure you put aside time each week to do something you love.

▶ Identify a number of people you are interested in becoming friends with. If they are shy, begin to express interest in them. If *you* are shy, begin with a simple smile and work on finding some common ground.

▶ Create a challenge or a project for yourself. Work on it consistently until you can step back and admire the final product.

▶ Take responsibility for your own actions. Instead of blaming others, ask yourself what *you* could have done differently ... even if only a little bit differently.

▶ Visualize positive scenarios. Relax, close your eyes, and picture things the way you want them to turn out.

▶ Develop an interest or hobby by reading a book about it or attending a lecture or show on the topic.

▶ Read the news, don't watch it. Resist the temptation to look at negative images.

▶ Recognize sensationalism when you see it.

▶ Read books written by figures that you admire; they can be a window to your future.

9 780978 666316